*I Call You*
**Friends**

Other books by Patrick O'Sullivan SJ

*Prayer and Relationships: Staying Connected – An Ignatian Perspective* (2008)

'O'Sullivan companions his reader in an armchair conversational style of teaching, offering discussions, personal anecdotes and reminiscences. He flavours his teaching frequently with humour, but not to distract from imparting profound theological truths.' (*Catholic Leader*)

*Sure Beats Selling Cardigans: Fostering Our Relationship with God* (1995, fifth printing 2011)

'As soon as I began reading, the depth and scope of this book were strikingly evident … The chapters on prayer offer simple, practical advice, with anecdotal material that borders on the delightfully profane … One cannot but marvel at the way O'Sullivan presents some of the most profound articles of our Christian faith.' (*Eremos*).


*God Knows How to Come Back Home: Reflections on an Active Spirituality for Today* (1999)

'Like St Ignatius, the writer believes that God can be found not only in the quiet solitude of the cloister but also in the hurly-burly of the marketplace, not only in contemplative prayer but also in practical and loving service of one's neighbour' (Brian Grenier CFC).

# *I Call You Friends*

## Friendship with Jesus in Daily Life

**PATRICK O'SULLIVAN SJ**

**Foreword by Andrew Hamilton SJ**

**David Lovell Publishing
Melbourne Australia**

First published in 2018 by
David Lovell Publishing
PO Box 44  East Kew
VIC 3102  Australia
*tel/fax* +61 3 9859 0000
*email* publisher@davidlovellpublishing.com

© copyright 2018 Patrick O'Sullivan SJ

This book is copyright. Apart from any fair dealing or the purpose of private study, research, criticism or review, as permitted under the Copyright Act, no part may be reproduced by any person without written permission. Inquiries should be addressed to the publisher.

Cover image: *Christ Giving His Blessing*, Hans Memling, 1478, oil on oak panel, 38.1 x 28.2 cm. Norton Simon Museum of Art, Pasadena CA. Courtesy Wikimedia Commons.
Design & production by David Lovell Publishing
Typeset in 12.5/18 Garamond
This edition printed through Ingram Spark

National Library of Australia card number
and ISBN  978 1 86355 169 4 (pbk.)

A copy of the Cataloguing-in-Publication entry is available from the National Library of Australia

---

*Acknowledgement*

Grateful thanks to the Australian Province of the Society of Jesus for their assistance with the publication of this book.

# Contents

| | |
|---|---|
| Foreword by Andrew Hamilton SJ | 1 |
| Introduction | 5 |
| God is love | 7 |
| Abide in my Love | 12 |
| Cycling with God | 14 |
| Forgiveness and love | 16 |
| Prayer of petition | 22 |
| Fasting | 24 |
| Do I look at or do I see? | 26 |
| ANZAC Day – A reflection | 29 |
| Women in the church | 31 |
| Prayer – some reflections | 33 |
| What we carry in our hearts shows in our bodies | 35 |
| Our Lady | 37 |
| Mary and Joseph | 42 |
| Banjo Patterson, Henry Lawson and St Ignatius | 44 |
| St Ignatius | 47 |
| Prayer and daily living | 50 |
| Life is a gift | 53 |
| Who do I belong to? | 56 |

# I Call You Friends

| | |
|---|---:|
| The present moment and eternity | 58 |
| Our words, our deeds, and integrity | 61 |
| The early church and the church today | 65 |
| Discernment – some reflections | 68 |
| Discernment from another angle | 70 |
| Listening – to ourself | 73 |
| Listening – to others | 76 |
| Jesus, Light of the World | 79 |
| Jesus, Light of our world | 82 |
| The Good Shepherd | 85 |
| Suffering and the cross | 88 |
| White martyrdom | 94 |
| An approach to the Paschal Mystery | 96 |
| The Mass | 99 |
| Reflection on the Resurrection | 104 |
| The Trinity and us | 108 |
| Jesus, Best Friend – *Anima Christi* | 111 |
| Appendix: The Examen | 113 |
| A select reading list | 118 |

*I call you friends,
because I have made
known to you
everything I have learnt
from my Father.*
John 15:15

# Foreword

One of the best descriptions I have heard of the place that prayer should have in our lives came from the mother of a priest colleague. I was talking to a women's group about prayer, stumbling in my attempts to reassure them that if they took prayer seriously they wouldn't always have to mind their tongues, be relentlessly earnest, consider themselves miserable worms, or leave their social world behind.

My friend's mother then came to my rescue, saying, 'So, what you mean is that prayer is important, but it's no substitute for a day at the races.'

'You've nailed it', I said, relieved.

When it comes to prayer, most of us need reassurance. We see all too clearly the poverty of our efforts to pray, the mediocrity of our lives, the cloud of distractions that eat away at our prayer like cabbage moths, the gap between our words and our actions, and the guilty knowledge that we often don't want God to come too close to us. We fear that instructions on how to pray will quickly turn into a list of our failures.

Like any good writer on prayer, Fr Pat O'Sullivan knows how we feel. In his book he writes colloquially, gives down-to-earth examples, is full of humour, and describes warmly and attractively God's relationship to us. He returns constantly to the presence and company of Jesus in our lives. He writes about serious things as a battler for battlers like you and me, and many of his best insights come in stories from other battlers.

His book is also about things that matter. Prayer is not the decoration on the cake but the flour that goes into its baking. In an earlier period, spiritual writers used to speak about solid devotion expressed in faithfulness to the constant demands made on us in everyday life. They distinguished it from a superficial and emotional faith. Fr O'Sullivan's book is solid, but never stolid.

Each reader will take away memorable lines, both solemn and quirky. My favourites are the children's explanations of love. One little boy said, 'Love is what is with you in the room at Christmas, if you stop opening your presents and just listen.' Another says, 'When someone loves you, the way they say your name is different. You know your name is safe in their mouth.' These lines open into mystery.

# Foreword

For most of us, prayer and reflection on our faith are necessarily like commercial breaks in the main program of our daily lives, The short reflections offered in this book are perfect for this, light at times, at other times touching life's harsh seasons with their sleet and storms, but always finding hope and energy.

Come to think of it, not a bad book to take with you to the races!

Andrew Hamilton SJ

# Introduction

In my previous books, the articles there have been arranged mainly according to the sequence of the different Weeks of the *Spiritual Exercises* of St Ignatius. In this book, there is no such sequence – the articles stand in their own right. A number of the articles have appeared in *Annotations*, the newsletter of the Christian Life Community in Australia; others also in *Madonna*. Readers who are familiar with the writings of the late Cardinal Carlo Maria Martini will see his insights popping up quite frequently – with grateful acknowledgment.

I have freely quoted from other writers, including Cardinal Basil Hume, Cardinal Hans Urs von Balthasar and G. K. Chesterton, presuming that some readers may not be familiar with their writings or the particular work quoted. But if the reader should be familiar, it is always a pleasure to meet up with an old friend!

Patrick O'Sullivan SJ

Easter 2018

# God is love

The hardest lesson to learn – and the easiest lesson to learn – is to let ourselves be loved. And when it is a question of Jesus loving us, the lesson becomes even harder.

We find a good example of this in the parable of the Prodigal Son. The younger son learns this lesson, but not the elder brother, who sees love as something to be earned – and ends up completely miserable.

An even better example, which Cardinal Carlo Maria Martini gives, is what happens to Peter during the Passion, when he betrays Jesus three times. After the third time, the gospel tells us, 'the Lord, turning, looked at Peter …' He just looked at Peter, just looked at him with love. '… and Peter broke down and cried'. It was then that Peter really learnt how overwhelming it can be, and yet how freeing it is, to let ourself be loved by Jesus.

This is a truth we know so well in our heads, but takes

# I Call You Friends

so long to move into our hearts. I offer the following quotes as examples of what has helped me in my journey, in the hope that others may likewise be touched.

> I want someone to know me completely, to understand me entirely, and someone to want me unconditionally. I want to be somebody's first choice, and I think the only one who knows me completely, understands me entirely, and wants me unconditionally, is God – and I am his first choice; and you are his first choice. The marvellous thing about God is that he cannot have second choices. He is limited that way! We are all first choices ... all the time.
> Cardinal Basil Hume, *Light in the Lord*

If God is not attractive to us, then we cannot desire him. The first step in our journey to him must be to turn towards him and see that he is good beyond all our imagining, that he is 'the joy of man's desiring'.
Gerard W. Hughes SJ, *The God of Surprises*

The deepest reason why so few of us are saints is because we will not let God love us.
Ruth Burrows, *Guidelines for Mystical Prayer*

God loves us. And God's taste is excellent. Whatever other people may think of us, God thinks a lot of us, and he's right. Sin consists in disagreeing with what God thinks of us: in saying, 'No, I'm really nothing to write home about, nothing worth doing anything about, nothing worth giving to anyone.' Sin is the failure to love ourselves as God loves us. It makes nonsense out of the beauty of creation and knocks the life out of everything.

Sebastian Moore OSB, *Before the Deluge*

In Matthew 22:34-40, Jesus tells us that we must love the Lord our God with all our heart, with all our soul, and with all our mind. This is the greatest and first commandment. And the second commandment is like it – we should love our neighbour as ourself.

In this passage, Jesus is not only talking about two commandments – he is also talking about three loves: love of God, love of our neighbour, and love of ourself. These three loves are only fully effective when they are inseparable. If one is lacking, the other two fumble around but they never really take off the way they can when the three are working together.

We all would know what love of God means. Jesus tells us – 'If you love me, keep my commandments.'

Another way of loving God is for prayer to be a regular part of our life. When prayer is a regular part of our life, it is a sign we want to spend time with Jesus, which is investing in the relationship. And that is a real act of love.

How do we love others? Simply by treating them the way Jesus treats people – with compassion, reverence and concern, as we see in the parable of the Last Judgment (Matthew 25:31-46).

How do we love ourself? There are different ways of answering the question.

For example, one quite profound way is to take the line, 'God comes to us disguised as ourself.' Rather enigmatic, but well worth the trouble of unwrapping.

One simple way for loving ourself is to be grateful. When we are grateful for our life, grateful for our gifts, grateful for all the blessings in our life, we are effectively saying, 'My life is good news!' And when we see and experience our life as good news, it is a sure sign we are seeing ourself as Jesus sees us – 'God saw that it was good' – and now God only sees us with the eyes of love.

But perhaps one of the best ways of loving ourself is to take seriously the Father's infinite and unconditional love for us in simple and practical ways. For example, I once heard a Josephite nun, of Italian background, tell of the crisis she had faced in preparation for her Confirmation when she discovered that all the children to be confirmed were expected to take the Pledge – the promise not to drink any alcohol until the age of 21.

In great distress, she went to her grandmother, her Nonna. Expecting a child growing up in an Italian family background not to drink wine would be like forbidding an Australian child to swear off Vegemite in their early years. Her Nonna listened to her problem, nodded, and then said, 'Darling, this is what you do. You stand up with the other children, you say the words, and then you wink at God!' What a wonderful image of the Father to live out of!

# Abide in my Love

In St John's Gospel (chapter 14), Jesus tells us that he is in the Father, and the Father is in him, and if we heed his words then he and the Father will come to us and make their dwelling with us.

How are we to understand this? Here's just a suggestion.

Some years ago I was at a gathering of young people, and, at one stage, a young Irish girl was asked to sing. She did, and the whole place became absolutely still.

The only way I could describe it would be to say it wasn't just a young girl singing – the girl *became* the song. The girl and the song were one, absolutely inseparable. The girl was in the song, and the song was in the girl.

Maybe it's something like that with Jesus and the Father. Jesus is the song of Love that the Father sings to each one of us, and, the more loving we become, there can be special moments when we, too, become the song.

Abide in my love

There is a well-known story about an actor, who used to give popular recitals, that fits well here.

On one occasion, after a well-received performance, the actor asked, 'Has anyone in the audience any particular request?' After some moments of silence, an elderly pastor, from the back of the hall, asked the actor if he would recite the Good Shepherd psalm. The actor paused for a moment and then answered, 'I will recite the psalm on one condition – that you recite it, too, after me.' The pastor, somewhat shyly, agreed.

The actor gave his recitation of the psalm and was greeted with enthusiastic applause. And then it was the pastor's turn. When he had finished, the whole auditorium was filled with a very deep silence – not a sound, no one stirred. The pastor bowed his head, feeling he had been too presumptuous. And then the actor broke the silence. 'You see the difference, my friends', he said. 'I know the psalm, but he knows the Shepherd.'

# Cycling with God

*During a recent annual retreat, I went to confession to a fellow Jesuit, and, for my penance, he gave me the following article to reflect on. It was titled 'Cycling with God'.*

At first I saw God as my observer, my judge, keeping track of the things I did wrong, deciding whether I merited heaven or hell when I die. But, later, it seemed as though life was rather like a bike ride. It was a tandem bike, and God was at the back, helping me pedal.

I don't know when it was that God suggested we change places, but life has not been the same since.

When I was in control, I knew the way. It was rather boring and predictable; I took the shortest route to travel between two points. But when God took the front seat, God knew delightful paths: up mountains and through

## Cycling with God

green gullies, through rocky places and all at break-neck speeds! All I could do was to hang on.

Even though it looked like madness, God said 'Pedal!' I was worried and asked, 'Where are you taking me?' God laughed and didn't answer and I started to learn to trust. I forgot my boring life and entered into an adventure. When I said, 'I'm scared!' God would lean back and touch my hand.

God took me to people who had gifts that I needed, gifts of healing, acceptance and joy. They gave me their gifts to take on my journey – our journey. And we were off again.

God said, 'Give the gifts away. They are extra baggage, too much weight.' So I did – to the people we met along the way – and I found that in giving I received, and still our burden was light.

I didn't trust God at first in control of my life. I thought God would wreck it. But God knows the secrets of bike riding. God knows how to balance, how take sharp corners, how to avoid rocks. And I am learning to shut up and to pedal to the strangest places. I'm learning to enjoy the view and the cool breeze on my face.

And when I'm sure I can't do any more, God smiles and says, 'Pedal!'

(Author unknown)

# Forgiveness and love

On the cross, Jesus prayed for those crucifying him: 'Father, forgive them; they do not know what they are doing.' We see clearly here that a forgiving attitude, like love, is at the heart of our faith. Moreover, Jesus tells us that unless we forgive others, we will miss out on the forgiveness the Father is offering us.

What does it mean to forgive someone? It does not depend on their apologising! Rather, it means I make a decision not to pass on to them any negativity in the way I think about them, talk about them, act towards them – no negativity in thought, word or deed. And that is a decision I can take, which can mean I still feel the hurt caused.

So often it takes time for our feelings to catch up – but that's OK. The Spirit always gives us time. I find the following prayer, found on the body of dead child at Ravensbrück Camp in northern Germany, where some 92,000

## Forgiveness and love

women and children died, a most inspiring example of forgiveness.

> O Lord, remember not only the men and women of good will, but also those of ill will. But do not remember the suffering they have inflicted on us. Instead, remember the fruits we have bought because of this suffering – our comradeship, our loyalty to one another, our humility, our courage, our generosity, the greatness of heart which has grown out of all this.
>
> And when they come to the judgment, let all the fruits that we have borne be their forgiveness.

To forgive is the prescription for happiness.
To not forgive is the prescription to suffer.
Holding on to what we call justified anger
  interferes with our experiencing the Peace of God.
Forgiveness means no longer living in the fearful past.
Forgiveness means no longer scratching wounds
  so they continue to bleed.
Forgiveness means living and loving completely in the present
  without the shadows of the past.
Forgiveness means freedom from anger and attack
  thoughts.
Forgiveness means not excluding your love from
  anyone.
Forgiveness means healing the hole in your heart
  caused by unforgiving thoughts.

# I Call You Friends

Forgiveness means seeing the light of God in everyone
  regardless of their behaviour.
It is never too early to forgive.
It is never too late to forgive.
For it is in giving that we receive.
It is in pardoning that we are pardoned.
Without forgiveness, you may not be forgiven.
(Author unknown)

Love, like forgiveness, is at the heart of our faith. Whatever we do, it is a great grace if we can do it with love – with a smile in our heart.

Justice without love is legalism – the letter of the law rather than the spirit.

An example of such legalism would be the occasion when the Pharisees criticised Jesus and his disciples for picking ears of corn on the Sabbath. Recently I came across a delightful counter-example. It goes back many years, to one of our Jesuit schools when corporal punishment was an accepted thing.

It happened in one of the classes that two boys were not doing the subject being taught: they were at the back of the class, playing cards. The teacher saw this and sent them up to the priest in charge of discipline to have them punished.

They told their story to the priest, who said, 'In future don't go to that class – just go for a walk in the park. But

## Forgiveness and love

you have been sent to me to be disciplined ...' And at that he went to his desk, took out a cane, and said to one of the boys, 'Put out your hand.' The boy did, and the priest placed the cane on the boy's hand. Then the priest said, 'Give me back the cane; and if anybody asks you, you can tell them I gave you the cane.'

Faith without love is ideology. We know our faith has degenerated into an ideology when we become judgmental and divide people into the goodies and the baddies. Faith unites, sin divides.

Hope without love is fanaticism. Love modifies hope to make room for questions. Without love there is no room for anyone who questions.

Forgiveness without love is manipulation. I recall one occasion when I was at a meeting and a lady said to me, 'Pat, I forgive you.' As she was someone I didn't know, I did not have a clue what she was talking about!

Courage without love is recklessness — like the saints who ruined their health through excessive austerities.

Generosity without love is self-indulgent extravagance. Some people have all sorts of wonderful ideas, and do all sorts of wonderful things in community — but often others have to clean up after them.

Care without love is cold duty. If we care for people without any personal investment, we are treating them as cases, not people.

## I Call You Friends

Fidelity without love is servitude. It is very sad to see old people who have become bitter. Once we stop laughing – that is a warning sign.

Honesty without love is brutality. Little children are often good at saying things the way they are, but, at times, not so good at saying them with love – as illustrated by the following story (warning: a little rough language).

A mother was working in the kitchen listening to her son playing with his new electric train in the living room. She heard the train stop and her son saying, 'All of you sons of bitches who want off, get the hell off now, 'cause this is the last stop! And all of you sons of bitches who are getting on, get your asses on the train, 'cause we're going down the tracks!'

The horrified mother went in and told her son, 'We don't use that kind of language in this house! I want you to go to your room, and you are to stay there for TWO HOURS. When you come out, you may play with your train again, but I want you to use nice language.'

Two hours later, the son came out of the bedroom and resumed playing with his train. Soon the train stopped and the mother heard her son say, 'All passengers who are disembarking the train please remember to take all of your belongings with you. We thank you for riding with us today and hope your trip was a pleasant one. We hope you will ride with us again soon.'

## Forgiveness and love

She heard the little boy continue: 'For those of you just boarding, we ask you to stow all of your hand luggage under your seat. Remember, there is no smoking on the train. We hope you will have a pleasant and relaxing journey with us today.'

As the mother began to smile, the child added, 'For those of you who are pissed off about the TWO HOURS delay, please see the witch in the kitchen.'

The language here may appear somewhat robust, but it is very much in keeping with some of the writings of the early Jesuits, like *The Christian Directory*, written by the Elizabethan Jesuit, Robert Parsons, and, according to its subtitle, 'shewing how that we should resolve our selves to become Christians indeede'. It has been said that this book, acclaimed by Protestants and Catholic alike, converted many more people to the Christian way of living than it has words. Because of its success, in some quarters it became affectionately known as 'A Spiritual Kick for Hard-Arsed Christians'.

At this time in the church, it would seem that Pope Francis, with his papal boot, is endeavouring to do just that. So, let us pray for Francis, that he may not be put off by those in the wings who keep calling out, 'Chewy on your boot!'

# Prayer of petition

Every so often we may come across the question of miracles and their credibility being raised. One common difficulty against miracles is that God can't change, as God is all-perfect, and so the idea that God listens to our prayers, and acts accordingly, is quite misleading.

There are different ways of speaking about God, and none of them can say it all because the Infinite cannot be contained in our finite language. In the language of the philosophers, God can't change because to change would mean to lose something God has, or to get something God doesn't have, but this can't happen because God is all-perfect.

However, we have to be very careful when we speak about God, because God is infinite while our words are finite. Whatever we say about God, we have immediately to add, 'But that's only partly true!' And so it is with saying God is changeless – it has to be immediately qualified. And what better way to qualify such a claim than to go to a higher power – the Scriptures.

Let me explain. In the Twelve Step program which deals with addictions, a crucial step for participants is to admit they are powerless with their addiction, and need to have recourse to a Higher Power outside their 'system'. This principle is one that Albert Einstein also espoused: 'No system', he said, 'can resolve a problem it itself has created.'

For example, if we are at a dinner party and break a tooth, the person we would go to to fix the problem would be a dentist, not the cook. We would go to a power 'outside the system'.

So, in this situation, to qualify the statement that God is changeless, we can go to a higher power, outside the philosophers' system – we go beyond the word of the philosophers to the Word of God, the Scriptures. According to the Scriptures, Jesus listened to people, heard their prayers, and healed them. Also, according to the Scriptures, Jesus is the image of the unseen God (Colossians 1:15). If the way Jesus loves us is a perfect image of the way God loves us, then we have an image of a God about whom we can truly say that God listens, and cares, and answers our prayers – although not always in the way we might expect!

# Fasting

Fasting has a long tradition in the church, no doubt inspired by Jesus' fasting in the desert before he begins his public ministry.

There is no doubt that in affluent countries like Australia there is an over-emphasis on food – TV programs on cooking are very popular, dieting is more than a fad, obesity is a problem with young children, junk food is condemned and yet grows in popularity. And so the story goes, in spite of the fact that in many parts of the world people are starving.

Perhaps if there were more emphasis on fasting, taken in the broad sense of the word, this might do something to help change people's attitude to having less rather than more. The following reflection has some practical suggestions in this regard:

# Fasting

Feast on unity. Fast from differences.
Feast on compassion. Fast from judgment of others.
Feast on listening. Fast from idle chatter.
Feast on goodness. Fast from perfectionism.
Feast on trust. Fast from anxiety.
Feast on pardons. Fast from grudges.
Feast on affirmation. Fast from gossip.
Feast on nature's beauty. Fast from pollution.
Feast on quiet moments. Fast from frenzied activity.
Feast on gratitude. Fast from discontent.
Feast on involvement. Fast from complacency.
Feast on the positive. Fast from negativity.
Feast on a good book. Fast from television.
Feast on humility. Fast from boasting.
Feast on forgiveness. Fast from resentment.
Feast on hope. Fast from despair.
Feast on our gifts and talents. Fast from jealousy.
Feast on love. Fast from fear.
Feast on acceptance. Fast from complaining.
Feast on gentleness. Fast from harshness.
Feast on God's Providence. Fast from fear of the future.

(Adapted from a prayer by
William Arthur Ward (1921-1994)

# Do I look at or do I see?

St Ignatius suggests we begin our prayer by recalling how the Trinity see us – not by recalling their presence, though that is implied, but how they are present, how they see us. They are not just looking at us, they really see us. And that makes a world of difference.

Cardinal Carlo Maria Martini sees a good example of the distinction between 'looking' and 'seeing' in the incident of the lady washing Our Lord's feet in Simon the Pharisee's house (Luke 7:36-50). My own private exegesis of the incident is that she was the woman taken in adultery, in John 8:1-12. She had obviously met Jesus previously in a way that changed her life.

In the course of the incident Jesus says to Simon, 'Simon, see this woman.'

Simon was just looking at her; he hadn't really seen her. And because he hadn't really seen her, he was quite

## Do I look, or do I see?

unaware of how he'd never seen Jesus, either. The main focus of Simon's vision was first of all himself, the generous host; then Jesus, an interesting oddity who could be quite entertaining; and finally the woman, a gross embarrassment. But Jesus gets Simon to really *see* the woman, and that turns the whole scene upside down – it is the woman who is the gracious host, and it is Simon who, as a host, is a gross embarrassment.

When we really see people, it means we do not take them for granted – as happened in the following story. The story is about an American pilot in the Vietnam War who, after many sorties, was eventually shot down. Fortunately he had time to bail out, but nevertheless he ended up a prisoner of war for six years.

Some years later, back in the USA, he and his wife were out dining one night when a man from a neighbouring table caught his eye, came across to him and said, 'Aren't you Flight Lieutenant So and So, from the aircraft carrier Such and Such? And weren't you shot down on your last sortie?' The pilot was extremely nonplussed, and asked, 'How do you know me and what happened to me?' The stranger replied, 'I was on that carrier, too. I was in supply. I packed your parachute.'

Later that night, the pilot searched his memory and

recalled the times he had bumped into the man on the carrier but had never bothered to speak to him. He had never really seen him as someone worth engaging with, because the man was just a rating while he was a star pilot. The man had saved his life – and the only recognition he had shown him was to take him for granted.

One helpful way of learning to really see people and not take them for granted is to bear in mind what Pope Francis has said:

'There are three phrases that should be part of every family:
>
> Please.
> Thank you.
> I'm sorry.' [1]

---

[1] General audience, 13 May 2015.

# Anzac Day
# A reflection

One of the better aspects of our Australian ethos is that our favourite song is the story of a born loser and our favourite national day celebrates not a victory but a defeat.

In other words, it really is a great blessing to acknowledge our limitations. That stops us from taking ourselves too seriously, and so leaves room for the Spirit to blow.

Anzac Day does not glorify war. There is world of difference between killing for what you believe in and dying for what you believe in. On Anzac Day we glorify sacrifice, not war; we remember those who gave their lives for what they believed in.

Anzac Day also reminds us of the important distinction between nationalism and patriotism. Generally speaking, nationalism is a menace; it promotes our policies and self-interest at the expense of other peoples. But patriotism is a virtue; it is a love for our people and our country, gratitude for the many blessings and gifts we have received and a willingness to share our blessedness with others.

These days a good question to ask is – which is the stronger, nationalism or patriotism? Unfortunately today I think we would have to say nationalism has the upper hand, especially given our policy with regard to asylum seekers. But – let us remember Gallipoli! What began as nationalism has been converted into patriotism. People who were once our enemies are now our friends. The bonds between our two countries are very deep, based on reverence for the dead and respect for the living. A wonderful example of the Spirit of Jesus taking over.

So, it is important to pray that the Spirit of Jesus will turn our hearts, and the hearts of our leaders, from nationalism to patriotism, so that Jesus can truly say to us, 'I was a stranger, and you took me in.'

# Women in the church

John Paul II once told us that we won't see the true face of the church until women have found their rightful place. There is much to endorse what the Pope has said, especially if we look at the way we men have handled authority.

The apostles were obsessed with authority. They were constantly arguing as to who was the greatest; and, from all accounts, this sort of power struggle is still going on in the Vatican, much to the disgust of Pope Francis. But authority was never an issue with the women who followed Jesus. And when the chips were down, the women were the faithful ones who stood by Jesus. It would seem that it is men who are not too good at handling authority!

One possible way to rectify this imbalance is to recall – and foster – the truth that there are two basic models of the church, the Marian model and the Petrine model;

and the Marian model, according to John Paul II, takes precedence over the Petrine model.

The Petrine model is based on the hierarchical and mainly visible structures of the church – pope, bishops, priests, sacraments, and so on. The Marian model sees the church as Mother, fostering the inner life of her children, and cherishing each one.

Cardinal Hans Urs von Balthasar has written that if the Marian dimension is denied or abandoned, 'the church becomes functionalistic, soulless, a hectic enterprise without any point of rest, estranged from its true nature by the planners. And because, in this mainly masculine world, all that we have is one ideology replacing another, everything becomes polemical, critical, bitter, humourless and ultimately boring, and people in their masses run away from such a church.'

Let us pray that the Marian model of the church will come much more to the fore, under the guidance of Pope Francis, so that the church will find appropriate ways of including women in the exercise of authority, enabling the true face of the church to emerge.

# Prayer – some reflections

Some years ago, the well-known Cistercian Monk, Dom Eugene Boylan, wrote a book entitled, *Difficulties in Mental Prayer*. On hearing of this, one of his confreres is reputed to have said, 'It must be a very long book!'

When we go to pray, one question that always manages to niggle us is – why are we so easily distracted? The answer is because we are such a mystery, even or especially to ourselves, as to what makes us really 'tick'– which, really, is not a very helpful answer.

However, an observation. If the tenor of our daily life is that we let our imagination flow freely, then the chances of our reining it in when we want or try to pray are rather minimal. In this regard, a certain self-discipline is most helpful.

Years ago, when I was teaching at one of our Jesuit schools, I had to fill in a report on each member of each class I was teaching. Depending on how busy the other teachers were, it often happened that the comments of the other teachers were well in before it was my turn. Some of the teachers' comments were rather laconic – 'Could do better', 'Very industrious' – but occasionally one hit the jackpot: 'Has a first-rate, indeed, excellent, butterfly mind.' Not conducive to meditation!

Moving on, I find the following quote from Meister Eckhart most helpful:

> Being aware of God
> is not in your power, but his.
> God shows himself when it suits him,
> and hides when he wishes.
> So, even if you think you can't feel him
> and are wholly empty of him, this is not the case.
> Be still, therefore,
> and do not waver from your emptiness.

To quote a former colleague of mine, Frank Wallace SJ, prayer is an encounter, not a performance. It is all about God, not us. In fact, when we pray it would be quite appropriate to put a notice on our door: 'Quiet, God at work.'

# What we carry in our hearts shows in our bodies

Our Lord was extremely tactile. He touched lepers (Matthew 8:3); put his finger into a deaf man's ear and touched his tongue with spittle (Mark 7:33); covered a blind man's eyes with a mixture of mud and spittle (John 9:6); let a prostitute wash his feet with her tears (Luke 7:38); and hugged little children – perhaps cuddled might be an even better word (Matthew 19:13). All acts of love.

One of the reasons why Jesus was so tactile was because he was the Incarnation of God's love. His own heart was a revelation of the Father's heart; and what we carry in our hearts shows in our bodies. I have come across many examples of this.

Some time ago, one of the newly ordained priests from the seminary where I was stationed came along to tell me about his experience of hearing confessions for the first time.

The occasion was a group of children, making their first confession. The young priest telling the story said, 'A little girl came in, and after she had said her piece, I told her, 'Now, dear, I am going to give you a special blessing. I closed my eyes and held my hand out over her to give her absolution. I suddenly felt her little hand against mine – she thought I was giving her a high five! But then she realised I wasn't, yet still kept her hand there.'

The little girl intuitively picked up, through the touch of his hand, what the young priest was on about – that this was a Jesus moment, much more important than a high five.

The body is a poor liar, for what we carry in our hearts shows in our bodies. And if we carry Jesus in our heart, then our interactions with others will always build them up and never put them down. As Cistercian André Louf writes: 'It is right and normal that the body should be part of the spiritual adventure to which we are called … A genuine interior life can grow only through the body.'

# Our Lady

In the book of Genesis, after Adam and Eve have tasted of the forbidden fruit, we have the scene where God confronts the serpent and says, 'I will make you enemies of each other; you and the woman, your offspring and her offspring' (Genesis 3:15).

In chapter 2 of St John's Gospel, we have the marriage feast of Cana. When the wine runs out, Mary discreetly asks Jesus to intervene, and he replies, 'Woman, what is that to me and to you? My hour has not yet come' (John 2:1-12).

And at the end of the Gospel, when Jesus is dying on the cross, John says, 'Seeing his mother and the disciple he loved standing near her, Jesus said to his mother, "Woman, this is your son"' (John 19:26).

John uses this special Messianic word, 'woman', at the very beginning and the very end of his gospel, to draw attention to the fact that, in Mary, the promise of Genesis is fulfilled. Through Mary and her offspring, the power of evil is broken, and the world's salvation is unfolding.

> She was standing there, racked with distress. The wild darkness, blind, mute and terrifying, wept tears of distress all around Golgotha. O Christ, the day turned to darkness when they dragged you away. Your final breath snuffed out the light. And there she stood, the mother, near the gallows.
> 
> The mother, groaning in the shadows at the foot of the cross, was consoled, shafts of light illumining her silhouette. And while her haggard eyes wept tears of blood, she was overcome with joy as she thought, 'My Son is God! My Son is the Saviour of the world.'
> 
> Victor Hugo, from *Les Malheureux*, 1855

More than a hundred years ago, a man travelling in a train in France found himself seated next to someone who appeared to be a wealthy peasant with a rosary in his hands. 'Sir', the student addressed the old man, 'do you still believe that old stuff?'

'Yes', the other replied, 'I certainly do. What about you?'

The student burst out laughing and went on, 'I don't believe that silly stuff. Follow my advice: throw your rosary out the window and learn what science has to say about it.'

'Science? ... Maybe you could explain it to me?' replied the old man humbly, with tears in his eyes. The student noticed the emotion on the face of his travelling companion and, to avoid hurting his feelings further, told him: 'Please give me your address. I will send you some information.'

Then, glancing at the business card the man had taken out of his inside pocket, the young man fell silent. The card read:

Louis Pasteur, Director<br>Scientific Research Institute, Paris.

(Taken from the newspaper, Vers Demain,<br>Montreal, Canada)

The central mystery of our faith is the Death and Resurrection of Jesus. Mary is the Mother of our faith because she is the outstanding sign of what faith in Jesus' Resurrection really means for us.

The greatest challenge we all face is suffering and death. In the Old Testament, the book of Job tries to explain this mystery, but fails to do so. Job, the just man, loses everything. And how does the story end? He gets a new wife, a new house, new children, new flocks of animals – all his possessions are restored. But that is not really satisfactory; a new wife and children can never take the place of those we have lost.

But in the New Testament the story of Mary is quite different. She, the just woman, also loses everything – her Son dies abandoned on the cross. And how does the story end? Not in a restoration, but in the Resurrection.

For example, if we read the Gospel of Luke – Mary's Gospel? – we never see the slightest suggestion, in the light of all the stories of Jesus' childhood, that Mary after the resurrection misses Jesus, that she wants him back, that she wants him 'restored'. Why? Because she knew that in his resurrection Jesus was sharing his new life with her, and he was much, much closer than he had ever been while he was on earth.

Mary's whole life, then, is a message that when we are hurt, disappointed, when we suffer, in spite of the temptation, it is not helpful to long for a restoration of the happy days we have lost. A much more life-giving approach is to ask for the grace to see our suffering as Jesus coming closer to us, inviting us to believe more deeply in his resurrection, so he can fill us with his new life. Mary says to us: Restoration – never. Resurrection – always and forever.

G. K. Chesterton had a real fondness for Mary long before he became a Catholic. For example, Mary presides over the whole drama in his epic poem, *The Ballad of the White Horse* – the story of how King Alfred, at Our Lady's bidding, drives out the Vikings; an allegory of Christianity triumphing over paganism.

In his book about Western civilisation, *The Everlasting Man* (1915), he explains his devotion to Mary by referring to images of the Child Jesus and his Mother, where we see, as Chesterton puts it, 'Those holy heads are too close together for their halos not to mingle and cross.'

# Mary and Joseph

There is an old tradition in the church that, after Adam and Eve sinned, the gates of heaven were shut and no one could enter heaven. Good people who had died, like Abraham and Moses and so on, hung around in a sort of celestial waiting-room, called Limbo. But after his death, on the way to the Resurrection, Jesus went to this place to greet these good people, opened the gates of heaven and led them in.

The best part of the story that embellishes this tradition is that the first person Jesus met was St Joseph. Jesus gave him a big hug, and Joseph whispered in his ear, 'How is your mother?'

The language here is symbolic, of course, not to be taken literally. To take it literally would be like arguing about the sort of chair Jesus is sitting on when we say he is seated at the right hand of the Father.

So, what is the point of the tradition and the story? What is the truth behind it?

The truth behind it is that Jesus and Joseph had a unique relationship; that Joseph and Mary loved each other deeply; and that, because of the Resurrection, love goes beyond the grave.

Maybe I am speaking just for myself, but I rather think St Joseph is one of the great saints of our church we are inclined to take for granted. (I was born on 19 March, his feast day!)

My memory is rather shaky here, but I think it was theologian Ladislaus Boros who wrote of St Joseph: 'He was history's exile. He stood in the shadows all his life, with empty hands. Jesus was not truly his son; and Mary was not fully his wife. There was nothing, no one, he could call his own.'

All true, but the fact remains that Joseph was the model of manhood whom Jesus identified with. And there is a striking resemblance between Joseph's life, with his empty hands, and what Paul tells us of Jesus: 'Though he was in the form of God ... he emptied himself.' Like Father like Son, as it were!

# Banjo Patterson, Henry Lawson, and St Ignatius

As an Australian Jesuit, I feel quite chuffed that our two most famous and most loved poets have more than a soft spot for the ideals that meant so much to Ignatius in his relationship with Jesus – chivalry and honour.

As a young boy, I used to love reading Banjo Patterson's poem, 'The Boss of the Admiral Lynch'. It is a story set in one of the revolutions in Chile, where the president was ousted and his opponent and army took over. All opposition was quelled until they came to the city's harbour. The only ship in the harbour was a little gunboat, 'The Admiral Lynch', tied up at the wharf. As the army approached, the captain of the gunboat hoisted the flag of the defeated president.

The opposition were quite taken aback, but, because

they had won the battle, they were feeling magnanimous. They sent a message to the captain that if he would haul down his flag all would be well. The poem continues:

> He listened and heard their message, and answered them all polite,
> That he was a Spanish hidalgo, and the men of his race *must* fight!
> A gunboat against an army, with never a chance to run,
> And them with a hundred cannon and him with a single gun:
> The odds were a trifle heavy – but he wasn't the sort to flinch,
> So he opened fire on the army, did the boss of 'The Admiral Lynch'.

Shades of Ignatius and the battle of Pamplona, where he encouraged the troops to fight to the end, till he himself fell wounded, and the citadel fell with him.

Then there's Henry Lawson, and his poem, 'The Dons of Spain', written on the occasion of the Spanish-American War of 1898. The theme of the poem comes in the first verse:

> The national honour's the thing most dear to the hearts of the Dons of Spain.

And the poem concludes:

> Then here's to the bravest of Freedom's foes who ever with death have stood –
> To the men with the courage to die on steel as their fathers died on wood;
> And here's a cheer for the flag unfurled in a hopeless cause again,
> For the sake of the days when the Christian world was saved by the Dons of Spain.

Ignatius, Banjo and Henry are a rather unusual combination, but I rather think Ignatius has the last word – God is to be found in all things.

*A footnote.* It was my father who first introduced me to Lawson's poem. Initially Spain was excluded from the United Nations, being regarded, under Franco, as a 'warlike nation'. Subsequently, wiser counsels prevailed, and Spain was allowed to reapply for membership. However, its application had to be ratified by the members of the UN. At that stage my father was leader of the government in the Senate, and had to introduce the motion of accepting Spain as a member of the UN. Speaking in favour of the motion, my father's closing words were:

> Here's a cheer for the flag unfurled in a hopeless cause again,
> For the sake of the days when the Christian world was saved by the Dons of Spain.

The motion was carried.

# St Ignatius

St Ignatius is an interesting saint – quite different from the usual run of saints. With many of our saints, we have a tendency to tame them and blur the essential message of their life.

St Therese of Lisieux is a good example of this. We give her a bunch of roses, a sweet smile, and gloss over her experience of dark depression and her message of complete abandonment to God – heroic in the extreme.

Apart from being a difficult saint to tame, Ignatius is also an interesting contrast with someone like Francis of Assisi – one of the best loved saints in the calendar. When Ignatius was writing the Constitutions of the Society of Jesus which he and his companions had just founded, he would often have mystical experiences – visions – that led to tears of consolation.

In fact, the tears of consolation became so consistent that his doctor told him that if they continued in the same fashion, he would go blind. Now, if it had been Francis,

## I Call You Friends

it is a pretty safe guess he would have said, 'What does it matter as long as I love my Lord?' But Ignatius judged he would serve Jesus better if he could see what he was doing and writing the Constitutions; so when the visions came, he refused to look at them.

He had work to do – his was a mysticism of service.

Ignatius is a complex character. At times he could be quite strict, yet the Constitutions for his order are extremely flexible – full of qualifying phrases, so as never to obscure the Mystery of Jesus and the uniqueness of the individual.[2] One of his close contemporaries has written: 'Our father wanted us, in all that we did, as far as possible, to be free, at ease with ourself, and led by the particular grace given to each one.'

In short, devotion to Ignatius is an acquired taste, but it is one worth cultivating.

In my present work, from time to time I meet up with seminarians who want to talk about their journey. On one occasion a young seminarian brought up the subject of distractions at prayer, and temptations in general.

---

[2] Such flexibility is very much alive in the Society of Jesus today. As you enter our General House in Rome, there is a big statue of Ignatius, and at its base are the words (in Latin): 'Go set the world on fire.' And right beside the statue is a large fire extinguisher!

## St Ignatius

I asked him how he dealt with them, and he answered, 'Well, it all depends. I have found one good way for me to change the scene is to make up a football team (Aussie Rules!) of all my favourite saints, and what they were good at.'

Unfortunately, I can only remember a few of the saints and their positions. The Archangel Michael, a fierce contender, was centre half-back; and on the flank beside him was John Paul II, also strong in defence! Dominic was an elusive half-forward flanker, and John Vianney was in the back pocket to cut off the goal sneaks.

As the team built up, I waited anxiously for Ignatius to appear, but he didn't get a guernsey. When the full team had been picked, I asked, 'Who's on the bench?' The seminarian gave a big smile, and said, 'Didn't I tell you? Ignatius – he's the coach!'

The more I thought about it, the more I appreciated what a wonderful insight the young seminarian had hit upon. The coach is someone who reads the play and moves accordingly – a very helpful description of discernment in action and Ignatius' way of proceeding.

# Prayer and daily living

Broadly speaking, prayer is any activity that deepens our relationship with the Trinity. We can deepen our relationship with the Trinity in a number of different ways.

First, there is Formal Prayer. Here the focus is explicitly on the relationship with the Trinity, and giving time to the relationship – for example, through Mass, meditation, the rosary, and so on.

And then there is Informal Prayer. Here, our intention (what we have in mind) is to serve and promote the Reign of God, which indirectly deepens our relationship with the Trinity. For example, in a letter to one of the pioneer missionaries in the Far East, Ignatius wrote, 'If the country where you are tends to be less conducive to meditation than this part of the world, so much the less is there reason for extending meditation … Where there is a complete ordering of all to the divine service, everything is prayer.'

## Prayer and daily living

Another example of informal prayer is when our relationship with the Trinity is the motive for what we do. When the relationship is the motive for what we do, whatever we do deepens the relationship.

In formal prayer, what we do *is* prayer. In informal prayer, what we do *becomes* prayer, either through the intention or motive, or both. Formal prayer is explicitly relational; informal prayer *becomes* relational. But both deepen the relationship, and, in that sense, both are prayer.

There is yet another way in which what we do is prayer, even though we are not consciously praying, nor consciously intending to serve and praise the Divine Goodness, nor consciously motivated by our relationship with the Trinity.

This happens when, without consciously adverting to it at the time, we have the mind of Christ in the way we relate with others. Jesus' account of the Last Judgment (Matthew 25:31-46) makes this very clear, when the king separates the sheep from the goats.

The king will say to those on his right hand, 'Come, you whom my Father has blessed, take for your heritage the kingdom prepared for you ... For I was hungry and you gave me food; I was thirsty and you gave me drink ...' Then the virtuous will say to him in reply, 'Lord, when

## I Call You Friends

did we see you hungry and feed you; or thirsty and give you drink?' And the king will answer, 'In so far as you did it to one of the least brothers or sisters of mine, you did it to me.'

Here the virtuous have encountered Jesus in a way that seals their eternal destiny – the stakes could not be higher – and they have been completely unaware of the encounter! How to explain that?

The simple fact is, whenever we treat people with love, care, respect, compassion, we experience them the way Jesus does – we truly have the mind of Christ.[3] Jesus is the Way, the Truth and the Life. Whenever Jesus is the way we relate (that is, we have his mind in what we do), that is a Jesus event, and it deepens our relationship with him.

---

[3] 'Always consider the other person to be better than yourself, so that nobody thinks of their own interest first … In your minds you must be the same as Christ Jesus' (Philippians 2:3-5).

# Life is a gift

St Paul tells us that Jesus is the centre of creation: 'in him were created all things in heaven and on earth … he holds all things in unity' (Colossians 1). Granted, then, that Jesus' presence fills all creation, we might expect to hear whispers of his presence in our ordinary daily living.

For example, how often do we hear little children say, when something upsets them, 'It isn't fair!'? No one teaches them to say that; we don't have to! They have an inbuilt sense of truth and justice. Why? How? Because the Truth has triumphed and permeates all creation. 'I am the Way, the Truth and the Life.'

From their earliest years, we teach children to say, 'Please', and 'Thank you'. We often hear parents say to their children, 'What's the magic word?' This emphasis on a sense of gratitude is effectively saying, 'Life is a gift.' To see and experience life as a gift is to acknowledge the presence of the Giver – who is the Way, the Truth and the Life.

We all love happy endings! J. R. R. Tolkien writes: 'The peculiar quality of "joy" in successful fantasy can be explained as a sudden glimpse of the underlying reality or truth … It is a fundamental truth of our faith that joy finally triumphs over grief, and that is our destiny.' Jesus again – the Way, the Truth and the Life.

In the Gospel of Matthew; Jesus tells us that he is the fulfilment of the Law and the Prophets – 'Do not suppose that I have come to abolish the Law and the Prophets; I did not come to abolish, but to complete' (Matthew 5:17). This is another way of saying that Jesus is the fulfilment of all God's promises.[4]

It is interesting to see how many of our favourite fairy tales ride home on the back of one of God's promises. So many end up with the line, 'And they lived happily ever after.' Where does that idea come from? It has more than a strong affinity with one of the Beatitudes: 'Blessed are the pure of heart, for they shall see God.' People who see God are surely going to live happily ever after!

---

[4] 'The Son of God that we proclaimed among you … was never Yes and No: with him it was always Yes, and, however many promises God made, the Yes to them all is in him' (2 Corinthians 1:19-20).

## Life is a gift

When prayer and daily living go together, finding God in all things can happen in all sorts of different ways.

Some time ago I heard the story of an old man who turned up at one of our Catholic hospices in a very bad way. He was taken in and nursed back to a reasonable state of health and then discharged. One of the nurses had taken a particular interest in him and, as he was leaving, she asked him, 'Johnny, what are you afraid of?' He replied, 'Dyin' in the gutter.' Well', she said, 'we'll pray about that.'

Some months later, the old man turned up again at the same hospice; and this time it was pretty clear his last days had come. The same nurse who had looked after him before took over again, cleaned him up, got him a new pair of pyjamas, and set him up in bed. When he had settled down, the nurse said to him, 'Johnny, this is the end for you this time. How do you feel about it?' He gave a big smile, and said; 'There's gotta be a God, 'cos there ain't no gutter!'

God can be found in all sorts of unexpected ways. A medieval Irish poem has its own version of finding God in all things:

> To go to Rome:
> Great the labour,
> Little the gain.
> You will not find your King there
> Unless you bring him with you.

# Who do I belong to?

In the Gospel of Luke (16:1-13), Jesus tells us that we cannot serve two masters – God and wealth. This can give rise to a very challenging question: who do I belong to – the world or Jesus?

What would be one of the significant signs of belonging to the world? If the world really has a hold on us, the issue at stake would inevitably be disguised and 'socially acceptable'. One such issue, I would suggest, is the matter of resentment. It is quite acceptable to bear a grudge, and even seek revenge. But this is radically opposed to any idea of forgiveness. And forgiveness lies at the heart of our faith.

With regard to our belonging to Jesus, a very practical sign that we do is that we try to make life easier for the people we live with. I remember a nun I know very well

## Who do I belong to?

saying, 'You can tell when a meal has been prepared with love; it has a different taste about it.'

It may be that I can do very little, but, as long as I am doing it with love, I am helping Jesus build up the Kingdom of his Father.

# The present moment and eternity

In chapter 17 of the Gospel of John, we read: 'This is eternal life, to know you, the one true God, and Jesus Christ whom you have sent.'

Here the gospel is telling us that whenever we knowingly act out of our relationship with Jesus, or the Father, we are connecting with Eternity. In a very real sense, what we do will last forever.

How do we cultivate this sense of Eternity? How do we deepen our realisation that here and now we are experiencing some dimension of Eternity? If it is Eternity that gives such value to what we are doing in the present moment, on account of our relationship with Jesus, then the more we are aware of and invested in the present moment, the more we are connecting with Eternity.

So often we miss out on the present moment – our mind is either in the past or in the future. When we do

## The present moment and eternity

that, we undermine our sense of Eternity. The Examen[5] at the end of the day can help us to become more aware of the present. It also reminds us that we are on a journey – a journey that ends in Eternity.

There is a story told of a young woman who had been diagnosed with a terminal illness, and given three months to live.

As she was getting her affairs in order, she contacted her rabbi and invited him to come to her house to discuss certain aspects of her final wishes. Everything was in order and the rabbi was preparing to leave when the young woman suddenly remembered something very important to her.

'There's one more thing – I want to be buried with a fork in my right hand.' She went on to explain: 'In all my years of attending socials and dinners, I always remember that when the dishes of the main course were being cleared away, someone would inevitably lean over and say, 'Keep your fork.' It was my favourite part of the dinner because I knew something better was coming. So, I just want people to see me there in the casket with a fork in my hand, and I want them to wonder, 'What's with the fork?'

---

[5] See the Appendix, pp. 113-116.

## I Call You Friends

Then I want you to tell them, 'Keep your fork – the best is yet to come.'

So, the next time we reach for our fork, may it remind us, ever so gently, that the best is yet to come. We might even end up saying Grace!

# Our words, our deeds, and integrity

Jesus said, 'The scribes and the Pharisees occupy the chair of Moses. You must therefore do what they tell you and listen to what they say; but do not be guided by what they do: since they do not practise what they preach' (Matthew 23:2-3).

Here Our Lord is telling us that an infallible sign of discipleship – of our integrity – is when there is no gap between what we say and how we act; when, in fact, we lay ourselves on the line.

A good example of what I mean is the story of a friend of mine who was a colonel with an engineering background in the Australian army at the time of the Korean War. At one stage he was at the front line, preparing for the arrival of an American tank battalion, that had to negotiate a very steep incline. So, he and his men made

## I Call You Friends

a bridge for the tanks to cross over from one side to the other.

When the tanks arrived, the commanding officer took one look at the bridge and announced, 'There's no way I'm going to risk my tanks on that bridge.'

My friend remonstrated, saying he had worked out the weight of the tanks and the strength of the bridge, but the officer was adamant. 'Sorry, no go.' My friend said, very gently, but firmly, 'Look, mate, I know what I am talking about. I am going to go and stand under that bridge. You just give the orders for your tanks to roll.' Which he did. And the tanks rolled over.

Any decision that brings together what we say and what we do, so there is no gap between, is a Jesus event, because we are acting on the level of our integrity. And when we touch our integrity, we are acting out of our relationship with Jesus. Briefly, when we put ourselves on the line, we are acting on the level of our integrity, on the level of our truth, and the deepest truth in our life is our relationship with Jesus.

I also think that another sure sign of a person's integrity is when there is no gap between the person and their voice.

With the passing of years, I have become more at-

## Our words, our deeds, and integrity

tentive to peoples' voices. Maybe it started many years ago when I was stationed at St Leo's University College in Brisbane with an elderly Jesuit who had a number of quaint sayings. One of them I have never forgotten is: 'Some people use words to express their thoughts. Some people use words to conceal their thoughts. And some people use words instead of thoughts.'

What later confirmed this interest in people's voices was an occasion, quite a few years ago, when, with a young Jesuit, Steve, I went along to hear Brother Andrew, the General of the Missionaries of Charity – the male counterpart of Mother Teresa's sisters – speak about his experience in Vietnam after the fall of Saigon.

At question time, one member of the gathering sounded off, quite angrily: 'You've told us all about the evils of the North taking over, but you have not said one word about the corruption in the South before the North took over.' The atmosphere became electric, especially since some of Mother Teresa's relatives, substantial both in build and in number, rose from the back of the hall.

In response, Brother Andrew said very quietly, 'I was asked to speak about conditions in the South after the North took over. I am not ignoring your question, I just was not asked to speak about it. But I will speak about it if the people here would like me to.' Which, of course, no one did.

## I Call You Friends

On the way home, my companion and myself got talking about the evening, especially the angry intervention. My young friend said, 'What really impressed me about Andrew was that, when things got tense, his voice never changed. There was never any gap between him and his voice.'

When there is no gap between the person and their voice, they speak from the heart – which is another name for integrity.

Perhaps another illustration of what a person says being an expression of their integrity is when a person is so identified with their work that it qualifies their whole approach to life – that is, their work is not a job or a career but a vocation, so that their vocabulary for everyday living is moulded by this vocation.

For example, Professor James McCauley was Professor of English at the University in Tasmania, and at one stage in his life he was operated on for bowel cancer. As he was coming out of the anaesthetic, one of the doctors told him, 'Professor, we have had to remove half of your colon.' To which Professor McCauley replied, 'Well, I guess it's better to be a semi-colon than a full stop.'

# The early church and the church today

Although every passage of Scripture is written for our edification, it is not always clear why a particular passage has been chosen for our instruction. For me, the following passage from St John's Gospel is a case in point, so I have presumed to indulge in my own personal exegesis.

> Peter turned and saw the disciple Jesus loved following them – the one who had leaned on his breast at the supper ... Seeing him, Peter said to Jesus, 'What about him, Lord?' Jesus answered, 'If I want him to stay behind till I come, what does it matter to you? You are to follow me.' The rumour then went out among the brothers that this disciple would not die. Yet Jesus had not said to Peter, 'He will not die', but, 'If I want him to stay behind till I come, what does it mean to you?'
>
> John 21:20-25

## I Call You Friends

My interpretation is that the point of this passage is to let us know clearly how fragile was the base on which Jesus chose to build his church.

First, there is Peter, whom Jesus has just named head of his church. And Peter's fragile humanity clearly shines through. Not only is he full of curiosity, but it seems to be tinged with a touch of jealousy in relation to 'the disciple Jesus loved'.

This disciple apparently wanted to get into the act, as he followed Peter and Jesus. 'Peter turned', the gospel tells us, 'and saw the disciple Jesus loved following them.' But Peter won't have any of it – he won't allow a threesome to develop but maintains the twosome – himself and Jesus.

Shades of the green-eyed monster!

And then we have the phrase, 'the rumour then went out among the brothers …' 'Rumour' is a polite word for 'gossip'. Apparently the first Christians were accomplished gossipers, and like good gossipers, they usually got it wrong.

I find it very comforting to realise how fragile were the people on whom Jesus chose to build his church, because it is very much the same today. We, the church today, are also a very fragile lot, rocked by scandals. But Jesus has chosen us to be his church, not because we're good, but because *he* is.

## The early church and the church today

Jesus loves us to pieces, and has chosen *us* to help bring about his Father's Reign in the world, and that will never change because he loves us unconditionally.

# Discernment – some reflections

Let me first reflect on the personal level ... Each of us has a unique relationship with the Father. This relationship is our truth, our integrity.

Discernment involves being aware of our relationship with the Father, and engaging with the world around us in the light of this relationship.

When we engage with the world in the light of our relationship with the Father, there is an experience of ease, of connecting, of spiritual consolation. When our engagement is not an expression of our truth – that is, our relationship with the Father – there is an experience of dis-ease, of not connecting, of spiritual desolation.

And reflecting on the communal level ...

Just as each individual has his or her own truth, so

## Discernment – some reflections

does each community. A community's truth is the fruit of the members connecting freely with one another, on the level of each one's truth.

So, the question for discernment comes to be: will this proposition be an authentic expression of the community's truth? Personally I may not like the idea, but I still can experience the proposition as an authentic expression of the community's truth.

Thus, I am not 'voting' in favour of the proposition. Rather, my vote is my statement that I can experience the proposition as an authentic expression of the community's truth – I experience this proposition as maintaining the connectedness, the truth, of the group.

If all remain connected, the decision flows (spiritual consolation). But if one person holds on to his or her idea, this can break the connectedness of the group, and a heaviness will set in (spiritual desolation).

# Discernment from another angle

If we are good at something, and love doing it, we develop a nose for it, so it becomes second nature. We can see this quite clearly in the area of sport. If someone is really good at a particular sport, we say they're a natural; we talk of them as 'reading the play.' They don't have to work things out – they instinctively know what to do.

I think a similar thing may happen with great artists. Someone once asked Camille Corot, the famous French artist, how long a particular painting had taken him. Corot replied, 'An hour – and all my life.'

If we love life and are good at living, we develop a nose as to what leads to life, and what blocks it.

We pick up the difference between what is life-giving and what is life-preserving. Being good at living does not mean being a success. 'Success' is not a Gospel value. When someone asked Jesuit poet and activist Dan Berrigan how successful his protests were, he answered, 'Our vocation is to be faithful, not successful'. Being good at living means our heart is in the right place.

For discernment, then, we have to be in touch with our heart, and learn to be still. If our heart is busy, we won't pick up what's going on. Just as water has to be still to give a true reflection, so there will be no true reflection of reality if we are in turmoil.

As well as the above, a number of other factors are important for discernment to be a reality for us.

**Prayer.** First, we need a regular prayer life. My times for prayer need to be long enough for me to feel I am taking the relationship seriously – there have to be space and time to keep the relationship running.

If I only pray when I feel like it, my capacity to experience the Mystery of God is severely limited. A living relationship with Jesus cannot depend on my moods.

**Self-discipline** (mortification). The purpose of our life is built into the very cells of our body. Hence, a certain self-discipline is needed so that the intangible world of faith is not drowned out by the immediate attractions of the tangible. Moreover, we must be prepared to go out of our comfort zones for the sake of others.

## I Call You Friends

**Listening.** Listening is so important that it deserves a section to itself.

# Listening – to ourself

*An unexamined – unreflected upon – life is not worth living.*
                                              Socrates

If we do not stop to reflect on our life, then our life becomes a series of events that happen to us, rather than a journey we are actively and creatively making.

To flourish, we all need space. If trees are planted too close to one another, their growth is stifled. If we don't have or are unable to create our own space, our life becomes a matter of survival, not living. Real life is stifled.

One of the main problems of our times is the inability of people to sustain their space, and so their presence. How often do we have the experience of having a conversation with someone, and come away feeling, 'There was no one at home.'

There is a difference between solitude and loneliness. With solitude, I am at home with myself, quite content to be alone. But with loneliness, I am not at home with myself and so I am not really at home anywhere, or with anyone. I can be in the middle of a crowd and feel utterly lonely. The fact is, I'll never be at home with myself unless I learn to spend time with myself, unless I give myself space to be me.

The big difficulty is how busy we are. It is so helpful to realise the busier we are the more our lives become cluttered – we hang on to things, and so we lose our space.

The well-known Dutch Jesuit, Peter van Breemen, in his book *As Bread that is Broken*, tells the story of two Buddhist monks walking along a very muddy road, where they come across a young girl wanting to cross the road, but the mud is too much for her. So, one of the monks picks her up, carries across the road and puts her down on the other side.

His companion strongly disapproves, but he says nothing. At the end of the day, he can contain his disapproval no longer, and blurts out, 'You should never have picked up that young girl!' His companion replies, 'I put her down. You are still carrying her.' When we are always busy, our hearts become cluttered and we hang on to things.

How do we stop being always busy?' It comes down to what we really want. The fact is, we all end up doing what we really want to do. Maybe a better way to phrase

## Listening – to ourself

the question is to ask – how freely do I want to live ? – remembering that freedom is a journey. 'We are not free: we freely become so.'

If we want to take the path to freedom, one of the best ways is to set aside a little time at the end of the day and reflect on our actions and interactions – which, of course, is what the Examen is all about.[6]

A good illustration of how helpful the Examen can be is the Cherokee Indian legend of the two wolves. It is the story of an old Indian chief who tells his grandson about the battle that goes on inside all of us. He said, 'My son, the battle is between two wolves inside us all. One wolf is Evil – it is anger, envy, jealousy, greed, selfishness, resentment, pride, self-pity, lies, lust. The other wolf is Good – it is joy, peace, love, gentleness, compassion, justice, generosity, humility, patience, kindness, truth.'

The grandson thought about it for some moments, and then asked his grandfather, 'Which wolf wins the battle?' His grandfather replied, 'The one you feed.'

A good question we can always come back to is – which wolf have I been feeding today?

---

[6] See the Appendix, pp. 113-116.

# Listening – to others

Listening can be described as a loving attention to the other that allows the other to be fully and freely present. One opposite to listening is bullying. For the bully, the other person does not emotionally exist.

Listening is not just something we do; it can be a whole attitude to life. In fact, it is the feminine dimension of experience, and can be very healing.

It is important to remember that men and women have different consciousnesses. Generally speaking, men are more interested in facts, while women are more interested in relationships. For example, if a woman is telling a story and a man interrupts and says, 'Just give me the facts', the chances are the woman will feel she has been kicked in the stomach (From *Knowing Woman*, by Irene Claremont de Castillejo).

## Listening – to others

A friend of mine in charge of the lost property office for one of the airlines at Melbourne airport told me a story that bears this out perfectly. The story is about a very sharp businessman who lost a piece of important equipment. He wiped the floor with the underlings on the ground floor, who were very relieved to refer him to my friend. He stormed into my friend's office, and my friend said, 'Sir, could you tell me your story …?'

The man was only too happy to oblige. When he had finished, my friend assured him, 'Sir, if the parcel has been properly addressed, we are sure to find it.' And so the interview ended. The next day my friend rang up the businessman to see how things were. As he was ringing, he noticed on his computer that the package had been found and was delivered.

When the man answered, my friend introduced himself, and the man said, 'Well, I suppose you have rung up to say you were right; the package has been delivered.' My friend said, 'Actually, sir, I have rung up to see how you were, but I am delighted the package has been found.'

There was a long pause, and then the businessman said, 'You know, yesterday I tried to get angry with you, and I couldn't. Do you know why?' My friend could only say, 'No, sir.' The man continued, 'because you really listened to my story.'

## I Call You Friends

When we really listen to a person, we are effectively saying to them that their story is worth telling because it is worth listening to.

Many years ago, when I was a Jesuit superior, my assistant said to me, 'Our men will always do what you tell them. But make sure you listen to them, because if a man feels that he has not been listened to he will carry a wound for the rest of his life.'

Listening is not easy. Unconsciously we can resist, because, if I really listen to another person, I may have to change my opinion. And we all resist change.

# Jesus, Light of the World

*Cardinal Carlo Maria Martini, hailed by Pope Francis as a 'prophetic figure' and a 'man of discernment and peace', gives us a reminder in the following extract:*

The symbols of light and darkness are a recurrent theme in the Scriptures; and light is a most appropriate symbol for God because we don't actually see the light; rather, it's because of the light that we can see everything else.

So, it is not surprising that Jesus tells us that he is the light of the world. It is only when we are in the light that we become aware of shadows: there are no shadows in the dark. In other words, it is only when we have a relationship with Jesus that we become aware of the shadows in our heart.

This happened to Peter, after the miraculous draught

of fishes, when he said to Jesus, 'Depart from me, Lord, for I am a sinful man.' Furthermore, we don't have a direct vision of Jesus; rather, because of our relationship with him, we can see and experience everything else as it truly is, that is, in its proper context.

A person who walks in the light, on account of their relationship with Jesus, has some idea of where they are going, which becomes clearer the closer we get to Jesus.

But life is a journey, and we can stumble and fall and bump into things, and maybe temporarily get lost in a shadow. But at least we know that the things we bump into are obstacles, and the shadows are real shadows that shut out the light. And as long we keep our relationship with Jesus running, we never quite lose our sense of direction. But if a person walks in complete darkness, this becomes clearer and clearer to everyone around them – except themselves.

What are some of the signs of a person walking in darkness? They walk at random, they walk badly, they constantly change their ground when challenged, and they have no constant point of reference. They will talk of their problems, but they are never satisfied with any solution because they constantly project onto others their own lack of an inner direction.

Nothing that is said to such a person is ever satisfactory because they have grown to love their state of confusion. They gradually become a little bitter, sceptical, and eventually they come to see any choice as plausible and worthwhile, because they don't believe any choice is really worth while. That is the situation of darkness. And it can lead to inertia, or to a hive of activities – because, when we can no longer distinguish between what is worthwhile and what isn't, any choice is as good as another.

# Jesus, Light of our world

We only see things truly if Jesus is at the centre of our heart – if we see and experience things in the light of our relationship with him. He alone, at the centre of our heart, can guarantee us the space and the freedom to love everyone and everything else in our life, in a life-giving way.

If anything else crowds out our relationship with Jesus, and becomes the centre of our heart, it is only a question of time before that created reality takes up all our space and blights all our other relationships, so that we lose our sense of perspective, our freedom, and become fixated. And the categories of success and failure become all important!

If I engage in any venture, without any reference to my relationship with Jesus, so that the venture has a meaning and purpose of its own, independently of my relationship, then the ultimate meaning of the venture will depend on whether or not it succeeds

But if Jesus is at the centre of my life for anything I do, so that the basic context for any venture, any experience, is my relationship with him, then the whole quality of my life changes. My life becomes a partnership with Jesus. And when that happens, the categories of success and failure take second place.

If my life is a real partnership with Jesus – in the sense that my relationship with him gives purpose and meaning to my life, to everything I do – then any enterprise is to be judged meaningful not because it succeeds but because it enhances my relationship with Jesus.

In practical terms, what exactly does it mean to have Jesus at the centre of our heart, so that our life is a real partnership with him?

It means that, whatever I do, I talk to Jesus about it, on the level of the heart. I tell him, as a real friend, how it affects me – my fears, hopes, anxieties. When I do that, I create space for Jesus in the centre of my heart, so that when my heart, with all its frailties, is engaged in this or that venture or concern, there is space for Jesus right in the middle of it.

A good time to practise this conversation would be at the end of the day, if we are in the habit of doing a daily

## I Call You Friends

Examen,[7] reflecting on the day to see how our relationship has been running.

Ignatius expressed what I have talking about in a very paradoxical way – so paradoxical that many people have removed the paradox to make it more manageable. And so we sometimes hear attributed to Ignatius: 'Pray as though everything depends on God; work as though everything depends on you.' Sound common sense, to be sure, but not too much room for the Mystery of God.

What Ignatius actually said was, 'Pray as though everything depends on you; work as though everything depends on God' – which is a very good way of combining the mystery of God with the mystery of the human person.

---

[7] See the Appendix, pp. 113-116.

# The Good Shepherd

I doubt if the parable of the Good Shepherd has an immediate appeal for us in Australia, given the size of the flocks of sheep we have grown used to. I remember the rather quaint story of a judge in Melbourne who invested in a small property on the edge of the city. To keep the grass down, he bought a few sheep. It happened to be a good season – the grass grew long and the sheep grew fat, with lots of wool. The judge decided to have the sheep shorn.

He duly took along his tiny wool clip to a wool broker, and asked about the current price of wool. A young clerk gave him a figure, and then asked, 'You have some wool to sell, do you, sir?' 'Yes', said the judge. Whereupon the clerk said, 'Give us your address, and we'll send round a couple of semi-trailers to pick it up.'

The judge gave a slight cough, and said, 'Actually, I have the wool in my car outside.' The clerk asked, 'How

## I Call You Friends

many sheep do you have, sir?' 'Three', was the reply. The young clerk leant across the counter, and said to the judge, in a very sweet voice: 'And what are their names?'

However, even though we may have to adjust our spiritual metabolism to take in the full import of the parable of the Good Shepherd, we must remember that in some parts of the world the image immediately rings true. A friend of mine, a nun in the USA, lives in a community that is part farm, part conference centre. The farm runs various animals, including a flock of sheep.

My friend has told me that a person's first impression of a flock of sheep can be that the scene is one of complete chaos, with so many sheep bleating and lambs running all over the place. But, as a matter of fact, everything is under control, because, when a lamb is born, the ewe makes a noise in the lamb's ear, and later on, whenever she makes that noise, the lamb comes running to her.

My friend also told me that, on a few occasions, a ewe has died giving birth, and she has picked up the new lamb and made a noise in its ear. And subsequently, whenever she went into the fields, and repeated the noise, the lamb would come running to her, which made caring for it very easy.

So, when Jesus tells us, 'The sheep that belong to me listen to my voice. I know them and they follow me', the image he is drawing on is a very rich one drawn from nature, and applies most aptly to our relationship with him. The whisper in the ear, and baptism, do have a lot in common!

Moreover, the matter of our recognising the sound of Our Lord's voice in our ordinary living is a very practical one, especially in relation to those occasions when we have done something wrong or hurt someone. Here, the genuine Christian response is to express our sorrow and regret, and move on into the relationship with Jesus. But, if we are not careful, the Bad Spirit can take over and we beat ourself up, blame ourself, and become very self-critical.

At these times, a very good question to ask is – is this the voice of Jesus? Is this the way Jesus speaks to his friends?' This inevitably puts the Bad Spirit back in its box.

# Suffering and the cross

Whatever is suffered in love is healed. There are two attitudes to suffering. We can see suffering as an evil that befalls us, to be avoided at all cost; or we can accept suffering as an integral part of our discipleship. St Paul reflects,

> Blessed be the God and Father of Our Lord Jesus Christ, a gentle Father and the God of all consolation, who comforts us in all our sorrows, so that we can offer others, in their sorrows, the consolation that we have received from God ourselves. Indeed, as the sufferings of Christ overflow to us, so, through Christ, does our consolation overflow
> 
> 2 Corinthians 1:3-6

## Suffering and the cross

Most of our prayers begin and end with the Sign of the Cross, to remind us that Jesus on the cross is at the heart of our faith. Because the cross is at the heart of our faith, it is also at the heart of our lives – our lives and our faith are inseparable. The cross is there for all of us. That is why it is so important to recognise the cross when it comes and accept it for what it is – an invitation to move beyond our comfort zones and go more deeply, in trust, into the mystery of an unconditionally loving God ...

*Prayer and Relationships*, p. 82

Suffering is not the problem; complaining about it is. Over the years, I have come across many reflections on this tremendous mystery. The following are some that have made the most impact on me:

> There are recesses in the human heart that were not there until pain came along to create them.
>
> Léon Bloy

> While human suffering makes us think God is absent, that may be because we have shaped God in our own image and likeness. The cross teaches us that the self-revelation of the true God, for whom humility is power, takes place in human weakness. The silence confirms that there is a God ... Vigorous poetic theological affirmations about the Word collapsing into a scream for the lost God have marked the Christology of Hans Urs von Balthasar.
>
> Raymond Brown

## I Call You Friends

It is important for spiritual progress to desire to sense at least a little of the mystery of the Son of God abandoned by the Father.

Cardinal Martini

Here is my Credo, the beliefs crystallised during the years when exposure to suffering has become an everyday experience, a part of life. I believe no pain is lost. No tear unmarked, no cry of anguish dies unheard, lost in the hail of gunfire or blanked out by the padded cell. I believe that pain and prayer are somehow saved, processed, stored, used in the Divine Economy. The blood shed in Salvador will irrigate the heart of some financier a million miles away. The terror, pain, despair, swamped by lava, flood or earthquake, will be caught up like mist and fall again, a gentle rain on arid hearts or souls despairing in the back streets of Brooklyn.

Sheila Cassidy, Sharing the Darkness

Only if Jesus is truly of God do we know what God is like, for in Jesus we see God translated into terms we can understand. A God who sent a marvellous creature as our Saviour could be described as loving, but that love would have cost God nothing in a personal way. Only if Jesus is truly of God do we know that God's love was so real that it reached the point of personal self-giving.

Raymond Brown<br>An Introduction to New Testament Christology

## Suffering and the cross

If Jesus were to come down from the cross, everyone would believe him. He certainly would reveal a powerful and successful God ... but he would no longer reveal a God who serves, gives his life for us, who loves us enough to strip himself of everything for love of us, even to the point of self-annihilation. Perhaps we always baulk slightly at this concept of God precisely because if we accepted it, we would have to change our attitude to life.

*Cardinal Martini*

In Vietnam, after the fall of Saigon, the future Cardinal, Nguyen Van Thuan, was imprisoned for thirteen years, eight of them in solitary confinement: a time when he could do simply nothing. He described to a friend a very low point of his imprisonment in these words:

> My morale was at its lowest. I was almost in despair. In the darkness of my cell, cut off from my diocese, from God's people, from any human contact, I could not do a thing for anyone; I could not even talk to anyone. I felt completely useless. I prayed, but God did not seem to hear. Then, all of a sudden I saw, as if in a vision, Christ on the cross, crucified and dying. He was completely helpless – certainly worse off than me in my prison cell. Then I heard a voice – was it his voice? – saying, 'At this precise moment on the cross I redeemed all the sins of the world.'
> 
> *Five Loaves & Two Fish*

## I Call You Friends

One of the messages of the cross is that, when we experience negativity in our lives, in whatever form it takes, we are not to transmit that negativity onto others but to take it into our hearts, like Jesus on the cross, and transform it so that it becomes a source of life for ourselves and others.

That is why prayer is so important. Transformation can only occur at the level of the heart. Unless our heart is engaged with Jesus, transformation can never occur.

As one Hasidic saying quoted by philosopher Martin Buber has it:

> Rake the muck this way: rake the muck that way –
> it will always be muck. Have I sinned or have
> I not sinned? In the time I am brooding over it,
> I could have been stringing pearls for the delight of heaven.

Finally, a word from Pope Francis, who warned of the risk of succumbing to the temptation of a Christianity without a cross, adding that 'there is another temptation – that of a Christianity with the cross but without Jesus.'

And he concluded,

> A church content with being well organised, and with everything lovely and efficient, but which denied the martyrs ... would be a church which thought only of

## Suffering and the cross

triumphs and successes, which did not have Jesus' rule of triumph through failure. Human failure, the failure of the cross. And this is a temptation to us all.

*Morning Homilies*

# White martyrdom

New ideas, and new ways of doing things have been popping up in the church from the very beginning and down through the ages – new ways of following Jesus and witnessing to his Gospel message.

Some have been rather quaint, like St Simon Stylites, who spent his life on top of a pillar (and rather irreverently has been named the patron saint of journalists, as he lived off a column).

But one idea I have come across recently – and I have no idea how widely spread it is – is the phrase, 'white martyrdom'. It is a phrase that goes back to the days of St Jerome, who used it of the desert hermits who aspired to martyrdom through strict asceticism.

Martyrdom is commonly associated with the giving of one's life for the sake of the Gospel. More often than not, especially in the early church, the giving of one's life

## White marytyrdom

involved the shedding of one's blood. And so the liturgical colour for the celebration of a martyr is red.

And this, I presume, has led to the idea of white martyrdom, as distinct from red martyrdom. For just as some privileged people witness to faith in Jesus by shedding their blood, so many, many ordinary people witness to their faith in Jesus in their daily living, through fidelity to his invitation to take up their cross and follow him.

Such fidelity in the ups and downs of daily life is costly. It is the cost of discipleship, in fact – which maybe is another name for white martyrdom.

# An approach to the Paschal Mystery

The older I get, the more uncomfortable I feel with an 'expiation' model of the Paschal Mystery, the model that suggests that Jesus' death was an act of expiation for our sins – that his death compensated the outraged justice of the Father.

Many still talk of Jesus 'paying the price of our redemption ... paying the debt for our sins.' However, who, on earth, did Jesus pay the price to? When our words completely lose touch with reality, and especially when they obscure the image of an unconditionally loving Father, it is time we moved on. So, I offer the following model as an alternative to the expiation model. It is full of presuppositions – but that is one way of dealing with mystery.

The Trinity have created our world according to an evolutionary process. Loss and diminishment are an

## An approach to the Paschal Mystery

essential part of the evolutionary process, which, in human terms, mean pain, suffering and sin.

In his book *On the Theology of Death*, Karl Rahner suggests that the act of death is a descent into the unity of creation: in death, the spirit breaks out of its present bodily limitations and reaches the place where there occurs the destiny – the self-development – of the world. Creation is a continuous event; at the moment of death (the moment of truth, when we see the whole plan of creation and our part in it) we go to the point of the act of creation, and so this is the opportunity for us to enter much more deeply into the reality of creation and participate more fully in its destiny.

When Jesus was on earth, he was subject to the limitations of space and time. In his dying he left behind the limitations of space and time and confronted the act of creation, and, through his resurrection, entered fully and completely into the whole of creation.

Jesus became part of the evolutionary process and so infused all creation with a new power, stronger than diminishment and sin – the power of his love. Left to itself, there was a certain finality about the law of sin and diminishment in the evolutionary process, but Jesus, through his dying and rising, becomes part of the process, absorbing the power of diminishment and sin to have the final word – and the final word is Love.

## I Call You Friends

St Thomas Aquinas says that the Divine Omnipotence must not be taken to mean the power to effect any imaginable thing, but only the power to effect what is in the nature of things. I take this to mean that the Trinity could not just wave a magic wand and clean up the whole mess. As St Leo says, 'We would have been incapable of profiting by the victor's triumph if the battle had been fought outside our nature.'

And Raymond Brown says much the same: 'The self-giving of God's Son changed human relationships to God, and thus transformed the cosmos.'

# The Mass

The Mystery of the Eucharist is such an extraordinary and unimaginable gift that there are many different ways of looking at it. For example, one of Jesus' favourite images of the Kingdom of Heaven is a dinner party:

> '… many will come from the east and west to take their places with Abraham and Isaac and Jacob at the feast in the Kingdom of Heaven.' (Matthew 8:11)

> 'The Kingdom of Heaven may be compared to a king who gave a feast for his son's wedding.' (Matthew 22:12)

> 'I shall not drink wine until the day I drink the new wine with you in the Kingdom of my Father.' (John 26:29)

But a dinner party was not just an image Jesus drew upon – it seems to have been a frequent event in his life:

## I Call You Friends

> On a Sabbath day he had gone for a meal to the house of one of the leading Pharisees ... (John 14:1-2)

> One of the Pharisees had invited him to a meal ...' (Luke 7:36)

> He had just finished speaking when a Pharisee invited him to dine at his house' (Luke 11:37)

> ... the Pharisees and the scribes complained, 'This man', they said, 'welcomes sinners and eats with them!' (Luke 15:2-3)

In fact, sharing a meal was so much part of Jesus' life that at his last meal with his friends he decided that the Last Supper would, in fact last for all time. And so we have the Mass – the family meal of Jesus' disciples – where people who believe in Jesus, and one another, come together to celebrate this common faith. In other words, in the Mass we celebrate our fellowship with Jesus and one another and so offer ourselves to the Father to help establish his kingdom.

At the Last Supper, Jesus said, 'Do this in memory of me.' And that is what we do. When we celebrate the Eucharist, we do what Jesus did, in memory of him.

Yet that is not all that happens. Not only do we remember Jesus, but, through the power of his Spirit given to the church, the memory comes true. Jesus becomes really present. And that is why the early Church Fathers were fond of saying that the Eucharist is a foretaste of heaven.

Just as in the Eucharist the memory of Jesus comes true, so, in heaven, all our dearest memories come true[8] – no moment of love, or truth, or goodness, or tenderness, or beauty is ever lost: in the end all is harvest. That is what the Eucharist foreshadows and guarantees.

It is also important to remember, as Timothy Radcliffe OP reminds us, that when Jesus gave us the Eucharist at the Last Supper, it was a moment of crisis. He was about to be betrayed, the community was about to fragment, all were about to desert him – and that was the moment he chose to give himself in the Eucharist. He transformed this moment of betrayal and infidelity into a moment of grace.

The Eucharist is the sign of the triumph of life over death, of hope over despair – the enduring sign that the Father's unconditional love for us is far, far greater than our human frailties. As St John tells us, 'God is greater than our hearts.'

---

[8] Or, as Karl Rahner says in one of his catchy phrases, 'Eternity is the enduring validity of our freely enacted past.'

# I Call You Friends

The feast of Corpus Christi celebrates the hospitality of God – we are always welcome at God's table, to share God's life.

Scripture scholar Brendan Byrne SJ has written that the hospitality of God is a constant theme in the Gospel of Luke, and it also appears in John. Jesus' first public miracle at Cana (John 2:1-11), where he produces 150 gallons of fine wine, is a gesture of great hospitality. And when Jesus feeds the crowds with a few loaves and fishes (John 6:1-13), the leftovers fill twelve baskets. Later in the same chapter, Jesus tells us he is the Bread of Life (6:25-40), and offers us himself in friendship. Later, as only to be expected, Jesus continues to embody the hospitality of God when he cooks breakfast for his disciples by the lakeside in Galilee (John 21:9-13).

With so much doom and gloom around us in these times, if we are not careful we can be led to think that the hospitality of God has dried up, since we don't seem to see much evidence of it. But that is not the case. The victory has been won – Jesus is the Lord of History, and his hospitality is showing itself, if we're open to seeing it, in its human face.

One of my nieces has a daughter, Olivia, who has Down Syndrome. Recently she and her husband were travelling to New Zealand, and they met up with another couple who have a little boy who also has Down

## The Mass

Syndrome. Naturally they started talking, and, at one stage, the mother told my niece that she had refused to have any tests before the baby was born. My niece asked her, 'How did you feel? What was your reaction when you saw your baby for the first time?' The mother replied very simply, 'I thought, well, he's come to the right place.'

The hospitality of Jesus is alive and well in those who come to his table, to be touched by his Spirit, so that they, too, may be a sign of his loving presence in our world.

# Reflections on the Resurrection

*Sometimes an article may appear on my computer, and I'm not quite sure where it has come from. The following is one such article.*

In John's account of Jesus' Resurrection, perhaps we may have wondered why he bothers to tell us that 'the cloth that had been over his head ... was not with the linen cloths, but rolled up in a place by itself' (John 20:5-7). The reason he does is quite significant.

In those days, in an ordinary Jewish household, there was usually a young servant to wait on the master of the house. At the end of the meal, when the master had finished, he simply crumpled up his napkin and left it on the table, as a sign to the servant to start clearing up.

But if he left the table without finishing his meal, he

would fold his napkin neatly and leave it in its place on the table, as a sign he was coming back.

Jesus was simply following the custom!

Some time ago, a friend sent me an email which was the result of a survey, conducted among a group of four to seven-year-olds, on the question, 'What is love?'

As you would expect, some of the answers were rather cute, like one six-year-old girl who said, 'Love is when you tell a guy you like his shirt, and he wears it all the time.' And some were quite profound, like one little boy who said, 'Love is what is with you in the room at Christmas, if you stop opening your presents and just listen.'

The one that appealed to me most was one little boy saying, 'When someone loves you, the way they say your name is different. You know your name is safe in their mouth.' Which is exactly what happened at the Resurrection, when Jesus appeared to Mary Magdalene.

In John 20:14-18 we read, 'As she said this, she turned round and saw Jesus standing there, though she did not recognise him, supposing him to be the gardener ... Jesus said "Mary!" She knew him then.' Though initially Mary did not recognise Jesus, the moment he said her name, she knew exactly who he was. No one said her name like Jesus. And no one says *our* name like Jesus.

# I Call You Friends

Maybe when we next go to communion, we might imagine and hear Jesus call us by name, because no one loves us like Jesus, and no one says our name like he does.

One notable feature about some of the Resurrection scenes is the number of times that Jesus appears to some of his closest friends and they do not immediately recognise him.

As we have just seen, Mary Magdalene thought he was the gardener. When he appeared to the disciples by the Sea of Tiberias, the gospel tells us, 'It was light by now and there stood Jesus on the shore, though the disciples did not realise it was Jesus' (John 21:4). Some verses later we have the enigmatic words: 'None of the disciples was bold enough to ask, "Who are you?" – they knew quite well it was the Lord.'

The disciples on the way to Emmaus did not recognise who their companion was until he broke bread with them (Luke 24:30-31). And when Jesus appeared to the Eleven, gathered with their companions, they thought he was a ghost (Luke 24:36-38).

Scripture scholars suggest that this common lack of recognition is that Jesus' closest friends and followers had known him 'in the flesh'; but now, after the resurrection, Jesus could only be known by resurrection faith. And it took some time for this transition from knowing Jesus in the flesh to knowing him by resurrection faith to occur.

It is a reasonably common assumption among Christian believers to think how wonderful it would have been to have known Jesus in the flesh when he was on earth, whereas we only know him now by faith. But the fact of the matter is, knowing Jesus by resurrection faith is a far deeper and more intimate way than knowing him in the flesh.

C. S. Lewis has a similar observation when he contrasts the situation of the first Christians with the Jewish Temple. To all appearances, the sacrifice in the Temple was the real thing – there animals were killed for all to see, blood flowed. By contrast, the Christian community's sacrifice centred around some bread and wine.

Lewis concludes: 'Yet the Christians had the audacity to maintain … that their innocuous little ritual meal in private houses was the real sacrifice and that all the slaughtering, incense, music and shouting in the temple was merely the shadow.'[9]

---

[9] *Christian Reflections*, p. 45

# The Trinity and us

Relationships are so important in our life because we are created in the image and likeness of God. In God there are three relationships whom we name Father, Son and Holy Spirit – the Holy Trinity.

Though we are created in the image and likeness of God, the big difference between us and the Trinity is that we *have* relationships – relationships are a part, a very important part, of who we are. But, in the Trinity, the Father, Son and Holy Spirit don't have relationships – they *are* relationships.

The Father does not have a relationship with the Son: he *is* the relationship of 'Father'. And the Son does not have a relationship with the Father: he *is* the relationship of 'Son'. This relationship between the Father and the Son is so vibrant that the relationship is also a Person: the Holy Spirit.

In a sense, then, the Trinity is all about relationships.

## The Trinity and us

Consequently, when the Trinity create us in their own image and likeness, our lives will inevitably reflect, in some imperfect way, the importance of relationships in our life. In effect, we are relational beings; and the more we are true to our relationships – that is, relate in ways that enhance the relationships – the more we are true to ourselves and experience the fullness of life that Jesus promises.

# Jesus, Best Friend

## The *Anima Christi* Prayer
## A modern version by David Fleming SJ

The *Anima Christi* is a popular fourteenth century prayer that St Ignatius included in his *Spiritual Exercises* and so was often attributed to him. It has had a number of different translations and interpretations and this one is among the most beautiful.

> Jesus, Best Friend,
> may your soul give life to me,
> may your flesh be food for me,
> may you warm my hardened heart.
>
> Jesus, Best Friend,
> may your tears now wash me clean,
> may your passion keep me strong,
> may you listen to my plea.
>
> Jesus, Best Friend,
> may your wounds take in my hurts,
> may your gaze be fixed on me,
> may I not betray your love.
>
> Jesus, Best Friend,
> may you call me at death's door,
> may you hold me close to you,
> may you place me with God's saints,
> may I ever sing your praise. Amen.

# I Call You Friends

*(previous page)* 'Jesus, Best Friend' is taken from David L. Fleming SJ, *Draw Me into Your Friendship: A Literal Translation and a Contemporary Reading of the Spiritual Exercises*, Institute of Jesuit Sources, 1996. In this book, David Fleming gives a literal translation of the Spanish original together with a contemporary interpretation drawn from his more that twenty-five years of experience with the *Spiritual Exercises*.

# Appendix

# The Examen[10]

The Awareness Examen, also known as the Examen of Consciousness, was one of Ignatius' favourite ways of praying. It is a very practical way for continuing the prayer of the heart and maintaining our motivation and zeal.

The most common form of the Examen involves five steps:

1. I recall how the Trinity see me – always with the eyes of love.
2. I thank them for their love and their gifts, especially for today.
3. I ask the Spirit for the grace to help me reflect on my day.
4. I look back over the day, again asking the Spirit to help me see what the Spirit wants me to see.
5. I look to the future, asking for the grace to deal better with my failures, and trusting in the Spirit to continue to guide and help me.

---

[10] Adapted from *God Knows How to Come Back Home*, pp. 43-48.

## I Call You Friends

It is easy for the Examen, at the end of the day, to become a mere formality, and so it can be helpful to vary how we approach it, as there are many variations of this basic format. Below are two such possible variations.

### First variation

1. An act of presence and gratitude to the Trinity
I begin by placing myself in the presence of the Trinity. I try to become aware of God beholding me … (Pause) … I thank God for my being and the Lord's constant presence with me.

2. I ask for what I seek and desire
With the Spirit leading me, I try to get in touch with what has been happening in me and through me today. I ask of the Holy Spirit an interior knowledge of the Lord's presence to me today.

3. Examination
I go through my day:
- events from the time of rising until now?
- what has been dominating my mind and heart today?
- experiences of satisfaction and dissatisfaction in my work?
- experiences of interpersonal relationships with others, whether of love or rejection?

– what interior experiences took place, of intimacy with the Lord, of consolation or of desolation?
4. With my new awareness
   – I speak to the Lord, seeking understanding and the meaning of these experiences, as well as the ability to recognise the Lord's constant companionship with me.
   – I make further responses to the Lord of gratitude or sorrow.
5. I close with an Our Father
   (adapted from the Canadian CLC Program)

**Another variation**

I place myself in the presence of the Most Holy Trinity.

I first turn to
*God the Father*
I thank you, Father, for my gift of life. 'It is good to be alive.'
I thank you, Father, for today – another day of life.
I ask you, Father, for light to see my day as you saw it.

Now I turn to
*God the Son – Jesus*
Jesus, where today did you walk with me?

## I Call You Friends

For what moment today, Jesus, am I most grateful?
Where today did I block your presence?
For what moment today, Jesus, am I least grateful?

Now I turn to
*God the Spirit*
Most Holy Spirit, be with me for tomorrow.
Help me to be open to your guidance
Glory be to the Father.
Glory be to the Son.
Glory be to the Spirit.
Now and forever.

# A select reading list

von Balthasar, Hans Urs, *Prayer*, St Ignatius Press, San Francisco, 1986.

Boylan, Dom Eugene, *Difficulties in Mental Prayer*, Scepter, Strongsville, OH, 1997.

van Breemen SJ, Peter, *As Bread that is Broken*, Dimension books, 1960.

Brown, Raymond E., *An Introduction to New Testament Christology*, Paulist Press, New York, 1994.

Brown, Raymond E., *The Churches the Apostles Left Behind*, Paulist Press, New York, 1984.

Burrows, Ruth, *Guidelines for Mystical Prayer*, Bloomsbury, London, 2007.

Byrne SJ, Brendan, *The Hospitality of God: A Reading of Luke's Gospel*, Liturgical Press, Collegeville, MN, 2017.

Cassidy, Sheila, *Sharing the Darkness: The Spirituality of Caring*, Darton Longman & Todd, London, 1988.

Chesterton, G. K., *The Ballad of the White Horse*, Cosimo Inc., New York, 2007.

Chesterton, G. K., *The Everlasting Man* (1915), Dodd Mead, New York, 1925.

Hughes SJ, Gerard W., *God of Surprises*, St Paul Publications, Middlegreen, Slough, 1985.

# A Select Reading List

Hugo, Victor, from *Les Malheureux*, XXVI, in *Les Contemplations*, 1855.

Hume, Basil, Cardinal, *Light in the Lord: Reflections on Priesthood*, St Paul Publications, Middlegreen, Slough, 1991.

Hume, Basil, Cardinal, *Searching for God*, Hodder & Stoughton, London, 1977.

Hume, Basil, Cardinal, *To Be a Pilgrim: A Spiritual Notebook*, St Paul Publications, Homebush, 1984.

Fleming SJ, David L, *Draw Me into Your Friendship: A Literal Translation and a Contemporary Reading of the Spiritual Exercises*, Institute of Jesuit Sources, 1996.

Lawson, Henry, 'The Dons of Spain', from *Popular Verses*, 1924.

Lewis, C. S., *Christian Reflections*, Wm B. Eerdmans, Grand Rapids, 2014.

Martini, Carlo Maria, *David, Sinner and Believer*, St Pauls Publications, Middlegreen, Slough, 1990.

Martini, Carlo Maria, *The Dove at Rest*, St Pauls Publications, Middlegreen, Slough, 1995.

Martini, Carlo Maria, *Ministers of the Gospel*, St Pauls Publications, Middlegreen, Slough, 1983.

Martini, Carlo Maria, *Through Moses to Jesus*, Ave Maria Press, Notre Dame, 1988.

Moore OSB, Sebastian, & Hurt OSB, Anselm, *Before the Deluge*, Newman Press, New York, 1968.

Nguyen Van Thuan, Francis Xavier, *Five Loaves & Two Fish*, facsimile edition, Pauline Books and Media, Boston, 2009.

Parsons, Robert, *The Christian Directory*, 1607, Scolar Press, University of Virginia, 1970.

## I Call You Friends

Patterson, A. B. (Banjo), 'The Boss of the Admiral Lynch', *The Works of Banjo Patterson*, Wordsworth Editions, 1995.

Rahner, Karl, *On the Theology of Death*, Herder & Herder, New York, 1961.

**PRAYER AND RELATIONSHIPS**
Staying Connected – An Ignatian Perspective
Patrick O'Sullivan SJ
215 x 140 mm  128 pp  pb   ISBN 978 1 86355 125 0

> *God the Father has his own personal space,*
> *and his favourite personal space is our heart.*

At the heart of our Christian calling, says Pat O'Sullivan, is the opportunity to share God's life, to be 'divinised', as Michael Casey has put it. We do this by allowing space for our relationship with God to unfold and develop.

This can be a task that is not too far out of our reach because it is God who has taken the initiative. God seeks us out, and offers us his life, his grace. We respond, or not. But if we choose to respond, we foster this relationship through our prayer. In doing this, we join with God's Son, Jesus, who took himself away from the hurly-burly of everyday to a place of quiet. We have an ally in our task. And, as Jesus himself reassured us, as we relate to him we also relate to his Father.

This book is an encouraging account of the way of prayer, and of fostering these relationships. It follows the sequence of the *Spiritual Exercises* of St Ignatius, though the author has chosen not to make use of Ignatian terminology. Thus it is approachable in its content and style. Pat O'Sullivan draws upon many years of experience as university chaplain, retreat giver, spiritual director and provincial of the Australian Jesuits to offer solid and helpful reflection. And the reader is often beguiled by his gentle humour.

Here is a book for 'pray-ers'. They will find much that is of help in their journey towards God.

**"SURE BEATS SELLING CARDIGANS"**
Fostering Our Relationship with God
Patrick O'Sullivan SJ
215 x 140 mm  176 pp  pb  ISBN 978 1 86355 046 8

This best-selling book has sold over 4000 copies in Australia and 5000 copies in translation in Taiwan and Japan. Out of print for a long time it is at last reissued with updates and a fresh new design.

All Christians are on a journey, a journey in faith and into faith. *The Spiritual Exercises* of St Ignatius Loyola present the stages people go through along the way of this journey.

Experienced spiritual director, retreat giver and writer, Fr Patrick O'Sullivan, describes these stages in an appealing, enlightening and light-hearted way. He shows how we approach the fostering of our relationship with God, looks at the shadows that cloud that relationship – sin – and how we move out of the shadows into light. At the heart of the approach is the truly human figure of Jesus, and the way we live out his Paschal Mystery in our lives. A final reflection on renowned fellow-Jesuit Pedro Arrupe is a tribute to one who has now completed the journey and whose life can show us the way.

Fr O'Sullivan's particular interest in the psychology of the person makes his reflections immediate and easily accessible to those who see spiritual growth as part of the general growth to maturity.

This is a book of practical, down-to-earth spirituality. Readers will find in it nourishment and encouragement as they make their pilgrimage towards the Kingdom.

**GOD KNOWS HOW TO COME BACK HOME**
Reflections on an Active Spirituality for Today
Patrick O'Sullivan SJ
215 x 140 mm 128 pp pb ISBN 978 186355 070 3

> *In God's creative act ...*
> *there is room for*
> *all the sins of the world,*
> *because God knows*
> *how to come home.*
>
> F. Rossi de Gasparis SJ

Up until the time of Ignatius, deep union with God was mainly associated with contemplative prayer in convents and monasteries. Ignatius showed that God can be found noy only in prayer but also in the marketplace, through a 'mysticism of service'. This kind of active spirituality, argues Pat O'Sullivan, needs three characteristics: it must

- maintain our motivation and zeal
- help us make sense of the darkness
- deepen our sense of Providence.

Ignatian spirituality, he argues, can bring all three together, and so help us find God in our everyday lives. We do not do this alone, but walk with others, and can act in ways that promote rather than impede their, and our own, journey to God.

And at the end of the journey, O'Sullivan says, we can make the epitaph for Ignatius' tomb our own: 'Not to be hemmed in by all that is great, yet able to be caught up in all that is small and tiny – that is truly divine.'

**Fr Patrick O'Sullivan** SJ grew up in Brisbane, Australia, where he was educated by the Christian Brothers. After school, he went to Melbourne to study for a Bachelor of Arts degree. In 1951 he joined the Jesuits, and was ordained by Cardinal Gilroy in 1962. He taught at St Ignatius' College, Riverview, NSW, and after ordination spent his tertianship in Paray le Monial, France. He completed an MA in Philosophy at Melbourne University, and later did a PhD in Philosophy at Queensland University.

His appointments have included Dean of Newman College, Melbourne; Dean and University Chaplain at St Thomas More College, Perth; Vice Rector and University Chaplain at University of Queensland and Rector of Students at Campion College, Melbourne. From 1973–79 he was Provincial of the Jesuit Order in Australia and then Secretary for the Christian Life Communities in Rome, followed by a stint as Pastoral Assistant for the Jesuit Refugee Service, East Africa.

While involved in the retreat ministry, he was also editor of the Jesuit magazine of spirituality, *Madonna*, for a number years, and his most recent post was as resident spiritual director of Corpus Christi Regional Seminary in Melbourne.

www.ingramcontent.com/pod-product-compliance
Lightning Source LLC
Chambersburg PA
CBHW071353080526
44587CB00017B/3087